Affirmations That Move the Throne Room of GOD

A 30-45 day journey of adjusting your mind toward GOD'S plans and desires for you

by Iris L. Jones

Also by Iris L. Jones

❖ One Simple Principle: I will give you the keys to the kingdom of Heaven, The Journey: Returning to your foundation in God

❖ Witty Sayings for the Winning Soul

❖ Effective Prayers that Avail Much

❖ Effective Warfare Prayers that Avail Much

For more information visit www.irisljones.com or www.kmowinc.com

Affirmations That Move the Throne Room of GOD
A 30-45 day journey of adjusting your mind toward GOD'S plans and desires for you

ISBN: 0615942598

Printed in the U.S.A.

Dedication

This book of affirmations is dedicated to all of my supporters, my family and the One who has taught me to "Let this mind be in me that is also in Christ Jesus"…Philippians 2:5; GOD. This book will help you to come into the prosperity of the mind, spirit and soul if you embrace the GOD within you and by faith, believe that "With GOD all things are possible." Matthew 19:26

Contents

Introduction

Affirmations That Move the Throne Room of GOD is a powerful 30-45 day self actualization practice that will help you change your way of speaking, thinking, and your response to others. The saying "Actions speak louder than words" will manifest in your life through your behavior as you change the way that you speak. The Bible provides insight into how powerful our words are. Matthew 15:18 reads "*But what comes out of the mouth proceeds from the heart…*"

While on a spiritual fast, the LORD spoke to me and instructed me to write this book to assist HIS people on their quest to "*Let their (your) mind **be** in them (you) that is also in Christ Jesus…*" This means that we are to practice not only living HIS example, but also demonstrating temperance through our response to the vocabulary that we use. Our words must match our actions, as this is a command from GOD (Matthew 12:37). This way, those of us who are spiritual will experience victories in the midst of defeat in the "world" because our words are dependent on who and what we believe.

Whose report will *you* believe? After reading and reflecting on the daily affirmations, you will journal your feelings and allow the healing transformation to begin. These affirmations will **MOVE the Throne Room of GOD for you**. Healing will come forth.

Iris L. Jones

Preface

Each day, ask the Holy Spirit to guide you as you read the affirmations, for this is how they will truly work for you. Also, read the page that you turn to. Perhaps, the LORD has a specific message for you. Just mark the page that you read, but if you keep turning to it on a daily basis, GOD may be telling you that this is an area that you should work on more intensively. Use your Bible; seek more closure from the WORD of GOD. Ask HIM to help you to *"lean not on your own understanding"* as you work these affirmations, so that you can experience a better life. Remove distractions out of your life, by casting them out of your existence. Your words are powerful…think about it. What things have you spoken that have happened?

Now, it is time to change the pattern whether your experience has been good or bad. If your experiences have been good, make them better. If your experiences have been otherwise, crack the code of defeat and accomplish victory. You can do it when your words align with your actions.

30-45 days is not a long period of time, but when you set your mind to do better, there are attacks that will come. Therefore keep your mind, body, soul and spirit covered by the power of GOD. Ask HIM to keep you strong, to build you up. Most importantly, pray, seek HIS face and fast if you need to. Fasting is needed more than ever these days. Just think, this book came as a result of a spiritual fast. What will come from you when you complete this 30-45 day quest?

PART 1
Days 1-30

Day 1
Affirmation for Trust

Because my time is in Your Hand, LORD I place trust in YOU. Because I trust you, I know that my outcome will be good. Because I trust in you, I know that I can trust others. I know that I am healed from past issues concerning trust. You are my trust who rescues me from the hands of my enemies and persecutors. Because I trust you I will not fail in my life because every failure is only preparation for my success. I will succeed in all that you place in my hands, because you trust me. Therefore, I trust you.

Journal: In what ways can I work on developing my trust in GOD? Do I trust HIM? Is my inability to trust GOD affecting my relationships with others?

Day 2
Affirmation for Independence

I shall live my life as a free being according to the will of GOD for my life. I am not bound by sins of the past, I am healed, forgiven and set free. Therefore no religion can entangle me. The Love of GOD that never changes binds me. I am free within my spirit. I will not use my freedom as a cover up for evil. I will do what is right as a servant of GOD. In this way, only "right things" can come to me. These "right things" are according to HIS Will, and HIS way. I am independent in GOD to live freely.

Journal: How do I know that I am truly free? What scriptures validate my freedom? Am I walking in that freedom now? When will I begin pursuing freedom?

Day 3
Affirmation for Restoration

I will take the high road of unlimited resources in GOD that will restore to me the years that the locusts have eaten, to make all things new concerning me that will lift me up before the Lion of Judah with a praise that cannot stop the influx of abundance stored up for me. I am restored in every area of my life. My actions will demonstrate restoration. My spirit within me will reflect the Spirit of my divine Source- GOD.

Journal: Am I over the attack of the locust? Do I believe that I can be restored in every area of my life? What can I do along with the guidance of GOD to receive complete restoration?

Day 4
Affirmation for Hope

I rejoice in hope because the GOD of hope fills me with all joy and peace in believing so that by the power of the Holy Spirit, I may abound in hope. Therefore I can never be hopeless because the hope of the LORD is within me. My life is full of purpose because of this hope and I will continue to embrace it. The LORD planned my life to give me a future and a hope. I will continue to place my hope in HIM. In that, I am assured by my faith that everything will work out.

Journal: Have I placed my hope in the LORD's hands? How can I place my hope in HIS hands and really release what has been bothering me?

Day 5
Affirmation for Forgiveness

I am willing to forgive so that I can unleash my breakthrough and the amazing power that resides in me. I call forgiveness forth NOW so that I can move on with my life. I am no longer bound by the behaviors of others. I choose the high place in CHRIST JESUS who instructs me to forgive 70 x 7 times. When I forgive, I am freed in my spirit. I no longer hold grudges and I give myself permission to forgive. I forget because CHRIST has washed all of my sins away and I am forgiven.

Journal: Why haven't I forgiven? How can I let go? Is there anything lingering in my consciousness that I have forgotten to forgive?

Day 6
Affirmation for Weight Release

I lift my eyes to the heavens and release every physical, spiritual or mental weight that is designed to hinder my progress. Whether I eat or drink, whatever I do, I do all to the glory of GOD. Whoever I have been carrying, I release NOW. I will not be anxious about my life, about my body or what I put on. My life is more than food and clothing, or carrying the burdens of others. CHRIST JESUS lifted my burden through HIS sacrifice for me. In that, I release every weight and remain on track.

Journal: What weight do I need to release? Can I humble myself in my eating and drinking habits? Am I carrying old things around with me in my mind or spirit? Are there things that I am hoarding?

Day 7
Affirmation for Successful Business

I can do all things through HIM who strengthens me. I am successful in business ventures. New contracts and contacts will come into my experience. My business will prosper, creating additional businesses. Just like the four rivers flowing in the Garden of Eden, business resources shall flow to me. I speak to my business rivers of Pishon, Gihon, the Tigris and the Euphrates to flow NOW in my affairs.

Journal: Am I prepared to start a business? Is this business something that I will remain dedicated to in spite of the results? How can I work towards being successful in my business ventures?

Day 8
Affirmation for Money

Money is not my source but the Cause of it brings wealth into my life. This Cause is GOD, for HE produces the effect. I never look at money as my source of power, for it is GOD who gives me power through HIM to get wealth. GOD is my Effect. Without me having a need, HE cannot be the cause for my effect. Therefore, HE is my Cause and Effect. I do not lack because I do not want. My supply of money comes from the Divine Source who is the Creator of money and wealth, GOD.

Journal: Do I need money to survive? How do I view money? Why do I feel a certain way when I do not have money? Do I have an understanding of money and its purpose in my life, according to GOD'S Word?

Day 9
Affirmation for Peace

I open my heart to you LORD because you look at my heart. Out of my heart flow the rivers of life. In your presence I feel peaceful energies, I feel renewed. I am energized by your presence. I can face anything that comes my way, in a peaceful way. My mind is set on peace. Before I respond to anything that will cause me to come out of character I seek You because You are Peace. I rest in You because You are in my heart. I feel comforted and unified with You in a way that is shown by my actions.

Journal: What role does "peace" play in my life? How do I find peace in the more difficult situations? In what ways can I practice peace in my relationships?

Day 10
Affirmation for Patience

I am constant in prayer and rejoice in hope that I demonstrate patience in tribulation. I remain steadfast in doing the Will of GOD therefore I am not anxious. I am content in my present state and overcome whatever comes my way by the patience that GOD has instilled in me. GOD is with me when I begin to lose hope and reminds me that in HIM there is hope. I refrain from growing weary and keep my mind placed on my rock of salvation, the one who gives me the faith to continue on the journey of life. Where I go, HE accompanies me and reminds me that patience will have its perfect work in my life.

Journal: In what ways do I demonstrate patience? Do I act out of disbelief that GOD will not help me? What ways can I trigger and eliminate impatience?

Day 11
Affirmation to Ignore Ignorance

I refrain from contact with individuals who display ignorance through their thoughts, words and actions. I do not argue or fight to get my point across instead I let the maturity of CHRIST within me handle the outcome. I am quick to hear, slow to speak, slow to anger because my FATHER controls my life. I do not misrepresent HIS Kingdom by responding in an immature fashion. My words and actions are filled with love, honesty and servant hood. I demonstrate knowledge and will not perish. I understand that I must continually ask GOD for wisdom.

Journal: In what ways do I consciously or unconsciously participate in ignorance? What will I do differently the next time that I encounter it?

Day 12
Affirmation for Wisdom

The Spirit of GOD within me is filled with wisdom. Before I make any decisions I seek wisdom. When I go about my daily affairs I rely on wisdom. When I need a breakthrough I depend on wisdom to help me. Wisdom is the principle thing in my life that helps me to make the best choices. My physical and spiritual houses are built on wisdom. Wisdom flows from my lungs through my throat and out of my mouth when I speak. I will continue to build upon the wisdom embedded in me and ask GOD for wisdom because HE generously gives it without reproach.

Journal: How have I acquired wisdom? What is my understanding of wisdom? Are the decisions that I make in my life demonstrative of wisdom?

Day 13
Affirmation for Safety

With GOD'S permission, my angels of safety surround me wherever I go. They keep me alert when I am driving or walking. They are with me on my flight and offer assistance to all parties involved in my travels. I am safe in my home, when I am with family and friends or when I am alone. Peacefully I lie down and sleep for the LORD makes me safe in my dwelling. My spirit is safe in GOD, I am protected from attacks and unexpected illnesses. I have on the whole armor of GOD and withstand any negative energy that comes my way. A haven of safety blocks and removes them.

Journal: Am I really safe? What does safety mean to me? How can I overcome the worry that I may not be safe? Which ideas make me feel safe?

Day 14
Affirmation for Right Connections

By faith, I believe that I make the right connections pertaining to my life, my family, my ministry, my business, my education, my profession and my goals. With GOD on my side, I know that HE keeps me protected from anything that is not in HIS Divine plan for my life. My right connections are miracle workers, they obey GOD. They represent the excellence of HIS Kingdom, they mean business. They are not self seeking. They reverence GOD in a way that their business dealings are legitimate. They are not slackers or thieves. My right connections are GOD sent.

Journal: What are some of the mistakes that I have made with past connections? Am I part of the blame? What is an ideal "right connection?"

Day 15
Affirmation for Romantic Love

I am a conduit of love. I am ready for romance in a way that demonstrates passion and dedication. I trust GOD to send the type of mate that is created for me. I deserve a loving, healthy, happy and romantic relationship. My expression of romantic love will extend outside of the bedroom. When I am blessed with my mate I am loyal, when I am away from my mate I remain loyal. My love is strong and I enjoy giving and receiving love. I deserve love and happiness. Therefore, I am love and happiness.

Journal: Can I see myself fulfilled in a loving relationship? Do I have the understanding that I am capable of being in a loving, romantic relationship?

Day 16
Affirmation for Credit

I am confident that whatever I have need of, that GOD will supply. When I submit an application for my credit to be considered I am approved. I manifest "YES" across my application. I am not denied because GOD approved me to have what I am applying for. My faith determines the outcome. GOD only allows me to have what I apply for because HE desires for me to prosper. I attain what my FATHER says that I can have. I maintain responsibility for what HE has allowed me to be approved for.

Journal: Does GOD really give me the ability to attain credit or is it my own doing? How do I know if GOD desires for me to have a loan, even if it is approved?

Day 17
Affirmation for Self Improvement

My attitude has changed in a more positive way. My outlook on life has shifted and I know that all things are improving concerning me. I am on the potter's wheel being shaped in a way that makes me unbreakable. I am being molded for my Master's use. My new look will speak success and not failure. My self-esteem has improved because I understand that I am created in GOD'S image. Therefore, I represent HIS perfection and though I am not perfect, I represent excellence.

Journal: Are there any areas in my life that need improvement? What progress have I made in the areas that I have identified as needing improvement?

Day 18
Affirmation for Abundance

My conscience is aware of the Inner Presence within me and is my unlimited Abundance. My Abundance is not limited because of the Spirit of Prosperity that lives in me. My consciousness is filled with the good of my Creator who is Abundance. I faithfully express that when I obey GOD and HIS commandments I am set high above all the nations of the earth. The blessings of Abundance come upon me and overtake me. I Am Abundance because GOD is. Whatever GOD is, I reflect HIM.

Journal: Am I conscious that the gift of Abundance is within me? How do I view abundance? Is abundance the reflection of material things?

Day 19
Affirmation for Victory

I am a victor. I win every situation regardless of what the physical experience suggests. My battles are fought for me in the heavens and my angels are on post for me. GOD assigns specific messengers to help me along the way and to give me strategies for victory. The LORD my GOD is the ONE who goes with me to fight for me against my enemies and to give me victory. No matter what I face I am strong because the ONE fighting for me is stronger. I remain steadfast and face every trial because I receive the crown of life and victory.

Journal: How do I view the challenges that I face? What does victory look like? Does a victorious person always win?

Day 20
Affirmation for Restful Sleep

When I sleep, GOD is with me to stroke my hair and affirms in my spirit that everything is alright. HE forms a shield of protection around me and the light that covers me attracts dreams that are comprehensible. My dreams give me pieces to a puzzle and I responsibly put them together. I interpret what it is that the LORD and HIS Messengers want me to know and I am at peace with the revelation. As I sleep I encounter rest and my rest is not rattled with the spirit of fear. I am fulfilled in my sleep because I am at rest with the LORD. I awake energized ready for the next assignment from GOD within me.

Journal: What energy am I carrying to bed with me? Do I reflect on things that may disturb me when I sleep? How do I determine if I have truly rested?

Day 21
Affirmation for Moving

GOD in me, move what is not a part of my purpose on this earth. I no longer procrastinate and I am on time when I am expected to meet a deadline. I face this procrastination by making the time to do what I need to do. I call on creative ways to appear and show me what I need to do in order to be more active in my life. My state of mind changes so that I can adjust to the changes that must be made in my life. My mind will continue to provide me with innovative ways to process what it is that I need to do. My brain is energized to move to the next assignment, challenge or goal with ease.

Journal: In what ways can I psych myself out to do something that would normally take me a long period of time to get around to? When can I find the time to do something different? What does "moving" mean to me?

Day 22
Affirmation for Overflow

My threshing floors are full of grain, my vats shall overflow with wine and oil. My home is filled with plenty, my spirit is filled with plenty, and my mind is filled with plenty. Nothing but overflow comes from me. In HIM, I experience overflow that cannot be contained. My windows are open and I have unlimited room to receive it. My words of overflow are prosperous. Miracles are found in the overflow of my life. My life is reflective of the overflow of GOD. I am overflow and overflow is me.

Journal: How has overflow impacted my life? In what areas of my life would I like to see overflow demonstrated? Do I really believe that I deserve overflow? If so, why?

Day 23
Affirmation for Career

My career is designed for me and I hold the responsibility to maintain professionalism as I flow in my GOD given gifts to assist others. Because I am divinely place in my career, I have no worries about a job. In fact, my career is my calling. I am called to this career and because of this I do not lack. Money will continually flow as I operate in my career because it is my passion. I efficiently perform the tasks of my career with ease. I prove my love of my career through my actions because I reap successful results. I am prosperous in my career because I am called to this position.

Journal: Aside from an education or money what is the difference between a career and a job? Do I believe that a career is a calling?

Day 24
Affirmation for Healing

I am healed because HE healed me. By HIS stripes, I was healed, I am healed and I cannot be otherwise. When I encounter situations that need healing I declare "I am healed because HIS stripes healed me before the affliction." I clear my spirit of energies that would attempt to tell me otherwise. I tell every adversarial disease to exit my life for I am healed. I AM that I AM said "Behold, I will bring to whatever it is health and healing and I will heal you and reveal abundance of prosperity and security." I am healed.

Journal: Do I believe that I am healed of any circumstance even though I may have to experience going through it? How can I constantly remind myself that I am healed?

Day 25
Affirmation for Abstinence

I abstain from anything that defies the power of GOD within me. My daily affairs and interactions are reflective of GOD. I am aware that others depend on me to help them see the benefits in abstaining from things not fruitful to the spirit and soul so I set an example. I am mindful of the things that I eat and drink and I consider if I am looked upon as a role model to those around me based on the decisions that I make. I remain aware of what is not pleasing to GOD and I keep my mind and spirit in tune with HIS desires for my life. I abstain from idols and stay atoned with my GOD.

Journal: Am I able to abstain from one of the most problematic weaknesses that you have? By taking small steps, how can I work on abstaining from something that hinders my personal growth and development?

Day 26
Affirmation for Power

I am full of power from on High. No form of powerless defeat can hold me down. I am powerful when I speak. I exemplify power, love and a sound mind. I do not submit my power to anyone because GOD is powerful in me. I can do all things because of HIS power that strengthens me. Daily, I am raised up by HIS power and cannot be deemed powerless. I am power. My life exhibits power, my actions are full of power. My testimony gives me power to overcome any obstacle in my path. There is a bridge of power that has been built for me to cross over any trouble placed in my way.

Journal: How can I express power in my life without being confrontational? Am I dependent on anyone other than myself to express power?

Day 27
Affirmation for Higher Levels in GOD

The Divine power of I AM surrounds me, so I can only go higher in HIM. GOD keeps me in a state of thankfulness. I can only go higher in HIM. I keep my mind on HIS Kingdom, I can only go higher in HIS glory. I consider meeting HIM daily in HIS throne room. I can only experience HIM in that higher place. I see myself in the mirror of GOD, created in HIS image, not concerned about societal views. I can only go higher in HIM. I press toward the mark of HIS goodness and mercy all the days of my life. Every day has a brand new mercy. I can only meet HIM in that high place. I keep my mind on the higher places in GOD. GOD elevate Yourself in me.

Journal: Do I believe that I can get to a higher place in GOD? How do I access HIM? I must consider the goodness of GOD. What does it mean to me, to experience HIM at a higher level?

Day 28
Affirmation for Emotional Strength

My emotions are strong because GOD is my strength. Where I am weak, HIS power in my life is made strong. I will not break down when adversity comes my way. I remind myself that I am energized by the power of the anointing on my life. My spiritual muscles are exercised regularly as I call on the GOD in me to arise. When HE arises, all enemies scatter. I am not anxious for anything. I patiently wait situations through because of the grace that GOD has given me to stay strong. I detach from connections that drain my emotions and affect my actions. I am emotionally strong and I firmly stand in the strength of GOD.

Journal: Are there any emotional attachments that I need to break? Do I believe that I am emotionally healthy. If so, in what ways?

Day 29
Affirmation for Guidance

Oh LORD, my shepherd send Your angels to guide me as I make important decisions. Keep me on Your path of righteousness for Your namesake. Lift me up on the solid rock from which You stand. Keep me grounded in You when I am faced with difficult decisions to make. Instruct me and teach me the way to go. I acknowledge you, I lean on Your understanding. I ask You for guidance in my thoughts because You give freely to those who ask. In faith, I ask You for help in every path that I take. Remaining upright before you is my ultimate goal. LORD, guide me on the path called "Straight."

Journal: Am I willing to accept guidance from others? Who do I turn to when I need advice about most of my decisions? Should I change those who I seek out for help?

Day 30
Affirmation for GOD'S Will

I give thanks in all things, for this is GOD'S will in CHRIST JESUS for me. I am conformed to the Kingdom of GOD for this is HIS will, which is good and acceptable and perfect. The GOD of peace equips me with everything good that I may do HIS will, working in me that which is pleasing in HIS sight, through CHRIST who Is glorified forever. I stay away from immoral things, for this is the will of GOD concerning me. HIS Kingdom come, HIS will be done in my life. I stay away from foolishness and understand what the will of the LORD is. I am in GOD'S will when I am obedient to the testaments of HIS sacrifices for me. I freely delight in doing HIS will, for HIS law is in my heart.

Journal: What questions do I have about GOD'S will for my life? Am I able to control any outcomes in my life and are they a part of HIS will for me? Do I have beliefs about GOD and HIS purpose in my life?

PART 2
Days 31-45

Days 31-45

Statistics prove that when someone reads and recites affirmations on a committed basis, positive changes begin to happen in their life. What changes do you expect in your life and are you ready to make changes so that your expectations will become a reality? Now that you have read through the affirmations for the past 30 days it is time to experience the prosperity that results from reading and practicing (meditating) on them. It takes 40 days for consciousness to realize a truth. That is why this book was written for you to read it daily for a 30-day period, and then follow through by dedicating yourself to selecting random affirmations in this book during the 14-15 day period (days 31-45). Select only one affirmation per day. Upon reading it and speaking it aloud, reflect on what it truly means to you. If you struggle with understanding a specific affirmation, ask the Spirit of Truth for guidance. Think about it like this, when you were in school if you did not understand a lesson you asked your teacher for assistance and he or she would revisit and reteach the lesson that you struggled with. It is imperative to stick with this system of reciting affirmations.

Some things to consider are your perception of yourself, your perception of others, and your perception of who created you. Do you believe that a loving GOD who grants you access to HIS throne room will help you? Do you believe that if you cleanse your spirit of past teachings and habits that you have acquired that you can truly embrace the reality of who you are?

Did you know that in the Book of Revelation that the throne room of GOD represents the power and the majesty of the one sitting there? With that being said, when you apply your faith to these affirmations and remain attached to the expected outcome, which is good because GOD is, you will move HIM to act on your behalf from HIS Throne Room.

During your 14 days of affirmative reading, reciting and writing, these will be the most intense days because patience is not taught, it is learned. Your patience will be tried and you will feel like you are losing a great deal, and you are. You are losing impatience and the fear that GOD will not move for you. You are losing the negative responses that you normally meet in situations, and this is only the beginning. GOD loves positive thinking and when you begin "*speaking things that be not as though they were*" people will try to convince you that "this is how life is and that is the way it will always be." When you do not see immediate changes you will need to hang on by faith. Eventually you will notice positive changes and growth occurring rapidly in your life.

There is nothing better than experiencing peace in your life that actually has a different meaning from "quiet." Your soul will bask in the presence of the Father and while you are human you will continue to learn by trial and error. However your response to situations will be different. You will find that you consult GOD more and more and seek HIS peace that surpasses all understanding. GOD is PEACE and it can be found in HIM. Seek, find and keep this hidden treasure so that you can access HIS throne with your affirmed spirit.

Hang in there because the challenge has not occurred yet. The challenge is when you have to release yourself from the beliefs of lack and limitation. Enough of the lip service, can you move HIM in HIS throne room with your affirmations? Can you move GOD in a way that HE says, *"This is my child in whom I am well pleased*?"* GOD will hear your newly initiated affirmative words and will answer expediently. When you enter into the workplace the countenance of your co-workers will reflect change. When you decide that you are ready to trust again, you will not face the drama that you have in the past because a lot of your paranoia will eliminate itself. You will no longer battle with the scripture *"Life and death is in the power of the tongue."* Not only will you pay closer attention to the words that you speak and the things that you think but you will pay attention to those behaviors in others.

As you begin the challenge, think about something that you have always wanted to conquer. Is it a negative thought? Is it a false belief? Is it an addiction or bad habit? Is it something that you want to redo in your life? What is it? One assurance is that whatever you wish to conquer, once you have allowed the affirmations to pierce your spirit, you will be willing to face them. Take baby steps toward that which you wish to overcome and your steps will get bigger. Soon, you will feel like you can climb any mountain in your life, or better yet speak to it, tell it to move—and it will. After all, your words will have power because you will view your mountains as a temporal challenge. The Throne Room will respond to your words because your demeanor has shifted to a place of positive thinking that says that GOD is in control. Yes, this is what it is all about—GOD controlling your life and nothing else. Anything else controlling your life is a stronghold.

The Challenge

The Challenge

Has your life changed as a result of you practicing these affirmations for the past 30-45 days? Review every affirmation that you have randomly selected again (from days 31- 45) and consider the thoughts that come to your mind about each of them. What blockages have you conquered when affirming your truth? Which affirmations require more work?

Now, begin to respond to these questions by writing. You have had so much bottled up inside of you for so long and now it is time to release it. Who knows, you may have a book inside of you that comes forth, as a result. The affirmations that you have practiced will move the throne room to give you the boldness to become an author. Do you believe that your life can change for the better?

What affirmations can you create? What comes to mind as you walk this journey of spiritual cleansing? As you release your thoughts and feelings through your writing, challenges will disappear—almost suddenly. Some challenges will take longer than others to clear from your psyche, but you will feel lighter, empowered and relieved! You will come into a deeper understanding of "*I can do all things through HIM who strengthens me.*" The challenge seems simple but it is not. Become familiar with the truth that in your weakness HE is strong. You can do it, GOD believes it and so do I. You are well on your way to a prosperous future with hope!

PART 3

Beyond the challenge

40 days of Transformation

40 days of transformation

Anything that happened in Biblical times that caused major change included the number 40. Noah led and mentored people on a boat for 40 days and 40 nights while GOD set things in order on HIS earth. Moses, led the people out of Egypt after 40 years of confusion and disobedience. As I stated on page 70, it takes 40 days for consciousness to realize a truth. You have to allow yourself to detox from toxic situations that are inclusive of lethargic, lazy behavior. When I began the 30-45 days of affirmations, I found the writing piece that followed the affirmation was the most difficult. As the author of the book, I found difficulty in facing many fears but I made the decision to face them because if I did not, how can I impact the lives of others?

So think, how can you impact the lives of others? I have a few suggestions. First you will begin to live drama free. You will not view difficulties in the same light. People will get a different response from you. They will notice that your conversation has shifted. You are no longer crying "Poor little me," but instead reflecting on your actions and saying "Why can't it be me?" Why can't I face this or that person or situation? Why can't I accept hearing the word "no?" You will begin to notice that you are no longer fearful of the word because you understand that something better must be around the corner. Now this is what you call self-empowerment; you do not need to depend on anyone but the GOD in you speaking to your circumstance. Dr. Loretta Standley says something very powerful in one of her books "And Who Are You?" It reads: "*I propose the reason why*

30-day programs have such a low success rate is because they are out of alignment with Divine Order. They fall short of the necessary of the 40 days for transformation to occur." Again, the number 40 will make a change in your life, so take the remaining 10-15 days after the 30 days of affirmations and allow the universe to help you to select a page or affirmation that you must reflect on. This is key to your survival. On the remaining pages you will find affirmations listed by specified areas to help you finish this journey strong. Imagine, being filled with words that salute the GOD in you, can only bring about positive results. Enjoy and here's to your total freedom!

Specific Affirmations

Wise Woman Affirmations

I am a wise woman.

I embrace who I am spiritually, naturally, psychologically.

GOD is mindful of me and has given me wisdom for understanding.

I am phenomenal in all of my ways.

I support other women who display their GOD given abilities in and through their spirits.

I am wisdom.

I make wise decisions that show that I rely on GOD.

I am a: **W**ise **O**pulent **M**anifesting **A**bundant **N**urturer

Public Speaking Affirmations

I receive a positive response from my audience.

With a genuine spirit, I connect with my audience.

My message is clear and my audience receives me.

I am courageous as I speak to my audience.

I flow with the energy of GOD as I share wisdom from above.

I speak with power, authority and clarity.

I speak boldly, delivering my message with simplicity.

I maintain humility as I speak to others and my body language demonstrates balance.

Spirit Affirmations

My spirit is willing and overrides the workings of the flesh.

My dreams are protected by the heavens; GOD grooms my spirit.

I am filled with the peace and tranquility that comes from GOD.

I allow the flow of GOD to control me.

I am filled with the miraculous spirit of the Holy ONE.

I embrace who GOD has anointed me to be.

My spirit clearly hears GOD.

I remain steadfast as my spirit grows and transforms.

Power-filled Affirmations

I am constantly expressing my greatest potential.

GOD in me expresses HIS power through me.

I am all-powerful through CHRIST who strengthens me.

I relax while GOD does all of the work in my life.

I am a powerful soul, a powerful mind and a powerful mouthpiece of GOD.

My divine purpose has caused me to find power.

Because my mouth is powerful, I speak life into existence. I am victory.

I am full of power from the Universe (GOD).

Angelic Affirmations

I tap into my true potential and my angels protect my secrets between me and GOD.

I take a deep breath and just let go. My angels are with me.

I am assigned loving angels that will not allow my foot to dash a stone.

I meet my angels on a daily basis.

My angels transmit my prayers to GOD while I sleep.

My angels help me to heal and transform.

My angels remind me that I am free because GOD has freed me.

All angels assigned from GOD watch and protect over me and my loved ones.

Career Changing Affirmations

I am preparing to change careers now.

I recognize that the opportunity to change careers is here.

My new career allows me to demonstrate growth.

Changing careers is a joyous, easy-going process for me.

I enjoy working with my new coworkers.

I love working in this new profession.

My new work environment is supportive and fun filled.

I earn an abundant salary at my new job. I am thankful for my career change.

Child Affirmations

State these affirmations with your child, or let them fill in the blanks.

I am a happy child because…

I am healthy.

I learn well educationally and personally.

I am a blessing to my family.

I am loved.

I improve in school by…

I respect my family and they respect me.

I am safe and sound. I have a great support system.

Millionaire Affirmations

I have talent and knowledge to create millions of dollars.

I provide ideas that are worth millions.

I release all past fears that have prohibited me from being a millionaire.

Millions of dollars flow to me easily.

GOD enables me to bless others with the millions that I make.

Businesses flow out of my creativity that makes me a millionaire.

I am grateful to be entrusted with millions of dollars.

GOD, the creator of wealth, gives me millions in wealth.

Inspirational Affirmations

I am a Divine inspiration of GOD.

GOD in me inspires the lives of others.

In everything is the hand of GOD. HE is always at work concerning me.

In silence I hear the whispers of the LORD.

I atone myself with everything that GOD is.

My soul burns with the spirit of GOD and keeps me clean from all evil.

The breath of GOD moves through my body and inspires my soul, spirit and mind.

GOD'S spirit embraces me and never lets me go.

Confidence Affirmations

I am proud of myself and all of the accomplishments that I have made.

I know that I am worthy of great things in my life and coming into my life.

I willingly learn from my successes and see failures as blessings.

Personally, I am secure in my thoughts and in my actions.

I am free from the motives or personal vendettas of others. I confidently release.

I choose to express a confident attitude to others.

By faith, I leap forward. I trust. I trust. I trust.

Confidently, I embrace the now and apply my faith. I have "Now faith."

Freedom Affirmations

Love rules my thoughts and my actions. I am not full of fear but I have freedom.

I willingly let go of fear and release freeing thoughts into my life.

My experiences demonstrate someone free of bondage. I am secure in GOD.

I am spiritually grounded in peace and my mind surpasses all wrong thought.

I am safe and of a sound mind.

I release all things connected to fear from my life.

Freedom is mine. Love is mine. Joy is mine. Abundance is mine.

I am no longer worried about the outcome. I am operating in the now.

Daily Affirmations

Today, I will do my absolute best and perform at my highest ability.

GOD will reveal HIMSELF in and through my performance.

I receive the many blessings that come my way today.

This is the day that the LORD has made and my affairs are taken care of by HIM.

I will set time aside to be kind, loving, silent and understanding.

I thank GOD for waking me up today. I will bless this day for it's a gift.

I choose to see every day as an opportunity to grow.

My day is blessed, favored and protected by the HOLY SPIRIT.

Achieving Goals Affirmations

In every goal that I attempt to make, I will learn a lesson and bless the outcome.

Everything that I do, I give it my best effort, my full attention and dedication.

The resources that I need in order to achieve my goals are finding me.

I focus on the next step to take and I am determined to succeed at my goals.

I honor my values and my vision in order to fulfill my goals.

My goals are approved by GOD. I seek HIM before I move forward in my goals.

I willingly devote my time and full energy to my goals. They are priority in my life.

The path leading toward me fulfilling my goals is clear.

Gratitude Affirmations

I am truly grateful for my life. I bless the LORD with an attitude of gratitude.

I give thanks continually for every area of my life. I am thankful in all things.

When I express gratefulness my world expands. There is nothing impossible to me.

My Creator breathes through my nostrils and gives me life. I am grateful.

I am grateful for every season of my life. I bloom, grow, manifest and learn.

My heart gratefully beats and says "thank you" to every aortic vessel and vein.

I am being changed into the consciousness of JESUS CHRIST and I am grateful.

Gratefulness begets grateful experiences. I attract grateful people into my life.

Flying Affirmations

Breathe. Inhale; exhale. As I board the plane I know that everything is alright.

I am calm as I travel by airplane.

I am a safe passenger and a host of angels protect me.

I am secure on the airplane and I am confident that the airline staff is trained.

I willingly rest during the flight. I am safe in the hands of GOD.

My angels calm me and assure me that I will have a safe take off and landing.

I release all fear of flying. I am not bound by fear. I am free from fear.

I am safe while I travel as well as the other passengers.

Health Affirmations

I choose to take care of myself. As a result, my health improves.

I become healthier each and every day.

I walk in the healing that GOD has ordained for my life. I am made whole.

I heal those who interact with me through positive dialogue and prayer.

My body is already healed. A space in my body flows with healing.

I am open to treatment that will bring healing into my life.

I show patience with my mind and body as it heals.

I am healed. I am complete. By HIS stripes I am healed and remain healed.

Conclusion
What we must learn from "40 days"

Conclusion

If you are a believer of JESUS CHRIST and you have studied the HOLY BIBLE, then you should get a better understanding of why 40 days are important to anyone's transformation. Reflect on the following verses of scripture:

"Then Jesus was led (guided) by the [Holy] Spirit into the wilderness (desert) to be tempted (tested and tried) by the devil.

And He went without food for forty days and forty nights, and later He was hungry.

And the tempter came and said to Him, If You are God's Son, command these stones to be made loaves of bread.

But He replied, It has been written, Man shall not live and be upheld and sustained by bread alone, but by every word that comes forth from the mouth of God.

Then the devil took Him into the holy city and placed Him on a turret (pinnacle, gable) of the temple (sanctuary).

And he said to Him, If You are the Son of God, throw Yourself down; for it is written, He will give His angels charge over you, and they will bear you up on their hands, lest you strike your foot against a stone.

Jesus said to him, On the other hand, it is written also, You shall not tempt, test thoroughly, or try exceedingly the Lord your God.

Again, the devil took Him up on a very high mountain and showed Him all the kingdoms of the world and the glory (the splendor, magnificence, preeminence, and excellence) of them.

And he said to Him, These things, all taken together, I will give You, if You will prostrate Yourself before me and do homage and worship me.

Then Jesus said to him, Begone, Satan! For it has been written, You shall worship the Lord your God, and Him alone shall you serve.

Then the devil departed from Him, and behold, angels came and ministered to Him." Matthew 4:1-11 Amplified Version

What these verses teach us is that even in HIS power, JESUS, being on this earth in human form, had to face the challenge of being HIMSELF. As the Son of GOD, HE should not have had to endure the tests and temptations that HE did, but because HE chose to live in the human existence, HE demonstrated what we would have to go through. Have you ever felt on top of the world, but knew that things had to change in your life? JESUS, is our greatest example of what the number 40 stands for because HIS test in the wilderness is proof of what we will endure when we commit to change. JESUS did not fall to the temptations of the world, even though some biblical pessimists suggest such. JESUS exemplified victory by forgetting who did what to HIM, or even what Satan tried to tell HIM. HE knew who HE was in spirit and in truth.

Do you know who you are in spirit and in truth? Are you willing to let go of anything that is hindering your walk at this point? This is not a religious question, but a spiritual one. What must you own, in order to be released from it? We have to move past the notion that "nobody's perfect" and strive for perfection. The mediocrities of the world and its mindset is that we will never "get it right" but as scripture says "I (we) can do all things through CHRIST who strengthens me (us)." Do you believe that you can live as closely to perfection as possible? I do and I believe that if you trust GOD to help you through this transformational process of your life that you will succeed. In fact, I know it.

About the Author

Iris Jones is the founder of Iris L. Jones Ministries, Inc., which is under the umbrella of Iris L. Jones Enterprises, Inc. and the ministry headquarters Kingdom Ministries of Wisdom, Inc., all based in South Florida. She holds degrees in English, Educational Leadership, and Divinity. She is the author and self-publisher of many best selling books, and travels extensively to share the wisdom that God has imparted into her.

Iris stands on the firm belief that "God is in control and has the final say in everything!"

For more information about Iris or to order her books or inquire of her services, please visit www.irisljones.com or www.kmowinc.com.

Order Form

For additional copies of *Affirmations that Move the Throne Room of GOD: A 30-45 day journey of adjusting your mind toward GOD'S plans and desires for you,* send your check or money order, plus shipping to:

Iris L. Jones Enterprises Inc.
PO Box 668952
Pompano Beach, Florida 33066
Email: info@irisljones.com
Website: www.irisljones.com or www.kmowinc.com

Quantity	Item	Price	Total
(Between 1-49)	Affirmations That Move the Throne Room of GOD	7.99	
		Shipping	
		Total	

Add $2.00 Shipping and Handling per item.

Name _____

Address_____

City _____ State_____

Telephone _____

Email _____

For bulk orders (more than 50 books) email us at info@irisljones.com

Our Corporation

For more information about Iris L. Jones Enterprises, Inc., speaking engagement requests, website concerns or our publishing services or products, please email us at info@irisljones.com or info@kmowinc.com.

Affirmations That Move the Throne Room of GOD: *A 30-45 day journey of adjusting your mind toward GOD'S plans and desires for you*

Manuscript Started: 12/17/2013

Manuscript Completed: 12/18/2013

Manuscript initially published: 12/20/2013

Book Release: 1/1/2014

Book Manuscript Revised, Re-edited & Completed: 4/1/2014- 4/4/2014

www.ingramcontent.com/pod-product-compliance
Lightning Source LLC
Chambersburg PA
CBHW071817020426
42331CB00007B/1519